Courting Johanna

Courting Johanna

Based on "Hateship, Friendship, Courtship, Loveship, Marriage" by
Alice Munro

Marcia Johnson

Courting Johanna
first published 2009 by
Scirocco Drama
An imprint of J. Gordon Shillingford Publishing Inc.
© 2009 Marcia Johnson
Adapted from the short story "Hateship, Friendship, Courtship,
Loveship, Marriage" by Alice Munro (Knopf, 2002)

Scirocco Drama Editor: Glenda MacFarlane
Cover design by Terry Gallagher/Doowah Design Inc.
Author photo by Helen Tansey
Production photos by Terry Manzo
Printed and bound in Canada on 100% post-consumer recycled paper.

We acknowledge the financial support of the Manitoba Arts Council, The Canada
Council for the Arts and the Government of Canada through the Book Publishing
Industry Development Program (BPIDP) for our publishing program.

Library and Archives Canada Cataloguing in Publication

Johnson, Marcia, 1962-
    Courting Johanna / Marcia Johnson.

A play.
ISBN 978-1-897289-46-4

    I. Title.

PS8619.O468C68 2009   C812'.6   C2009-904697-0

J. Gordon Shillingford Publishing
P.O. Box 86, RPO Corydon Avenue, Winnipeg, MB Canada R3M 3S3

Playwright's Notes

One of my highlights as the 2004 Blyth Festival playwright-in-residence was meeting Alice Munro at an opening night reception. I could not pass up the opportunity to tell her how much I loved her writing.

I had been reading Alice Munro collections since high school. The latest I'd read was *Hateship, Friendship, Courtship, Loveship, Marriage*.

My intention was to comment on each story in the order in which they appeared in the book. I started with the first and title story. Not only could I identify with Johanna's feelings of being an outsider, I also understood the restlessness and boredom that could lead Edith and Sabitha to pull such a mean prank. Ms. Munro then said: "I always thought that one would make a good play."

There was the slightest of pauses before I responded with, "Really?"

Ms. Munro said: "You should adapt it."

For the next five minutes or so, she had to convince me that she was serious. She told me to call her and that she would give me her agent's information. A few days later, I was on the phone with William Morris Agency in New York negotiating the rights to *Hateship, Friendship, Courtship, Loveship, Marriage*.

Four years later, I was sitting in Blyth Memorial Hall on opening night of *Courting Johanna*, the play based on that wonderful story. I only hoped that all the Munro fans in the audience would feel that I'd done it justice.

To say that translating this beautiful story for the stage was a challenge would be the greatest of understatements. When I write original material I start with a two-character scene and let the characters "tell me where to go." I knew that I could not be so careless with this piece.

I spent approximately six months tearing down the story; mapping the order of events and identifying which characters, besides the three women, should make it into the play. Even with all this care and attention, I somehow ended up veering from the original story with invented dialogue and a new character.

Fortunately, Blyth Festival Artistic Director, Eric Coates paired me with director Kate Lynch. I say fortunately, because she also happens to have excellent dramaturgical skills. She was able to show me the error of my ways and to point me in the right direction. The new character disappeared and the play now mirrored the same structure and chronology as the story.

I can't thank Kate enough for helping me to focus and also for coaxing beautiful performances from the excellent cast. Thanks also go to Eric Coates for commissioning the script. This would not have happened without the support of the Ontario Arts Council and its Playwright-in-Residence grant of four years earlier.

I cannot forget to thank Alice Munro for having the faith in me to interpret her words. I do not know what she saw in this playwright whose work she had not seen but that faith gave me the courage to write this play. It is an honour that I will never forget.

Marcia Johnson
July, 2009

Staging

The premiere of *Courting Johanna* was done in two acts, partly to accommodate a major set change. It may be done in one act. All programmes and publicity materials must acknowledge that the play is based on the short story "Hateship, Friendship, Courtship, Loveship, Marriage" by Alice Munro.

Pronounciations

Gdynia .... Guh DIN yuh or Guh DEEN yuh
Johanna .... Jo ANN uh (silent 'H')
Kenora .... Kuh NORE uh
Regina .... Ruj EYE nuh
Sabitha .... Suh BEE thuh

Marcia Johnson

Marcia Johnson has participated in playwrights' groups at Obsidian Theatre Company; Theatre Passe Muraille; the Siminovitch Prize Playwriting Master Class with Carole Frechette; a musical theatre master class with William Finn at Canadian Stage Company; Canadian Stage's BASH residency, Tapestry New Opera's Composer-Librettist Laboratory (Lib Lab) and Ontario Arts Council Playwright Residencies at Blyth Festival and Roseneath Theatre.

Her plays include *Late* (Obsidian), *Courting Johanna* (Blyth), and *Binti's Journey* (Theatre Direct / Manitoba Theatre for Young People). Her radio dramas include *Perfect on Paper* (Silver Medalist, New York Festivals), *Say Ginger Ale* (Finalist, Canadian Screenwriter Awards), *Wifely Duties* and *Living in Hope: The Viola Desmond Story*.

Also a librettist, Marcia's short opera *My Mother's Ring* with composer Stephen A. Taylor was nominated for a 2009 Dora Mavor Moore Award for Outstanding New Opera. She continues to work with Taylor on their full-length adaptation of Ursula K. LeGuin's novella, *Paradises Lost*, commissioned by University of Illinois / Champaign-Urbana.

Marcia teaches an introduction to playwriting class at Sheridan Technical Institute in Oakville, is on the board of Theatre Ontario, a member of Playwrights Workshop Montreal and Chair of the Women's Caucus of Playwrights Guild of Canada. She has been a professional actor in Toronto since 1983.

Production Credits

Courting Johanna was originally produced at the Blyth Festival, July 23–September 6, 2008, with the following cast:

JOHANNA .... Catherine Fitch
EDITH, MILADY .... Tova Smith
SABITHA, WAITRESS .... Lisa Norton
KEN, STATION AGENT, HERMAN .... Gil Garratt
MR. McCAULEY .... John Dolan

Directed by Kate Lynch
Set and Costume Design by Kelly Wolf
Lighting Design by Michael Walton
Sound Design by Todd Charlton
Stage Manager: Shauna Japp
Assistant Stage Manager: Rachael King

(l to r): Lisa Norton (Edith) and Tova Smith (Sabitha)

Prologue

Scene 1

A train station. JOHANNA is waiting to be served.
She wears a shapeless and drab coat. After a moment,
she rings the bell on the counter.

JOHANNA: I need to ship some furniture.

STATION AGENT: *(From off.)* Furniture? Well. Now. What kind of furniture are we talking about?

JOHANNA: A dining-room table and six chairs. A full bedroom suite, a sofa, a coffee table, end tables, a floor lamp. Also a china cabinet and a buffet.

STATION AGENT: *(Entering.)* Whoa there. You mean a houseful.

JOHANNA: It shouldn't be that much. There's no kitchen things and only enough for one bedroom.

STATION AGENT: You'll be needing the truck.

JOHANNA: No, I want to send it on the train. It's going out west, to Saskatchewan.

STATION AGENT: First you'll need the truck to get it to here from wherever you got it. And we better see if it's a place in Saskatchewan where the train goes through. Otherways you'd have to arrange to get it picked up, say in Regina.

JOHANNA: It's Gdynia. The train goes through.

STATION AGENT: How would you spell that?

JOHANNA: G D Y N I A. Gdynia.

STATION AGENT: What kind of nationality would that be?

JOHANNA: I don't know.

STATION AGENT: A lot of places out there it's all Czechs or Hungarians or Ukrainians. I'm only stating a fact. Here it is, alright, it's on the line.

JOHANNA: Yes. I want to ship it Friday—can you do that?

STATION AGENT: We can ship it, but I can't promise what day it'll get there. It all depends on the priorities. Somebody going to be on the lookout for when it comes in?

JOHANNA: Yes.

STATION AGENT: It's a mixed train Friday, nine-eighteen a.m. Truck picks it up early. You live here in town?

JOHANNA: 106 Exhibition Road.

STATION AGENT: Exhibition Road, eh? I'm not used to these new street addresses.

> *JOHANNA has her wallet out, ready to pay. He waves the money away.*

                Pay when you ship. Can't tell you the price 'til we know what we're dealing with, you understand.

JOHANNA: I want a ticket for myself on the same train. Friday morning.

STATION AGENT: Going same place?

JOHANNA: Yes.

STATION AGENT: You can travel on the same train to Toronto, but then you have to wait for the Transcontinental, goes out five-thirty. You want sleeper or coach? Sleeper you get a berth, coach you sit up in the day car.

JOHANNA: I'll sit up.

STATION AGENT: Wait in Sudbury for the Montreal train, but you won't get off there, they'll just shunt you around and hitch on the Montreal cars. Then on to Port Arthur and then to Kenora. You don't get off 'til Regina, and there you have to get off and catch the branch-line train. But I won't promise your furniture'll arrive when you do, I wouldn't think it would get in 'til a day or two after. It's all in the priorities. Somebody gonna be there to meet you?

JOHANNA: Yes.

STATION AGENT: Good. Because it won't likely be much of a station. Towns out there, they're not like here. They're mostly pretty rudimentary affairs. That'll be thirty-five fifty.

JOHANNA pays for her ticket with exact change. She turns and exits.

STATION AGENT: *(Calling out.)* See you Friday.

After a moment, JOHANNA returns.

JOHANNA: The furniture I'm sending. It's all good furniture, it's like new. Bird's eye maple. I wouldn't want it to get scratched or banged up or in any way damaged. I don't want it to smell like livestock, either.

STATION AGENT: Oh, well. The railway's pretty used to shipping things. And they don't use the same cars for shipping furniture they use for shipping pigs.

JOHANNA: I'm concerned that it gets there in just as good a shape as it leaves here.

STATION AGENT: Well, you know, when you buy your furniture, it's in the store, right? But did you ever think how it got there? It wasn't made in the store, was it? No. It was made in some factory someplace, and it got shipped to the store, and that was done quite possibly by train. So that being the case, doesn't it stand to reason the railway knows how to look after it?

JOHANNA: I hope so. I hope they do.

JOHANNA exits.

Scene 2

> *Milady Dress Shop. JOHANNA is in the fitting room, wearing a full slip, her socks and shoes.*

MILADY: *(Handing a suit to JOHANNA.)* You're in luck. This should be your size.

> *JOHANNA takes the suit and immediately looks at the price tag.*

JOHANNA: It's expensive enough.

MILADY: It's very fine fabric. It feels as light as silk, but it wears like iron. You can see it's lined throughout, lovely silk-and-rayon lining. You won't find it bagging in the seat and going out of shape the way the cheap suits do. Look at the velvet cuffs and collar and the little velvet buttons on the sleeve.

JOHANNA: I see them.

MILADY: That's the kind of detail you pay for, you just do not get it otherwise. I love the velvet touch. It's only on the green one, you know—the apricot one doesn't have it, even though they're exactly the same price. Mind if I take a peek?

JOHANNA: Peek all you want.

MILADY: Of course you'll need your nylons on and your heels. How does it feel? Comfortable?

JOHANNA: The suit feels fine. There's nothing the matter with the suit.

MILADY: Sometimes that's just the way it is. You never really know until you try something on. The thing is, you have a fine figure, but it's a strong figure and what's the matter with that? Dinky little velvet-covered buttons are not for you. Don't bother with it anymore.

Just take it off.

MILADY exits. JOHANNA goes into the fitting room and strips down to her slip. MILADY returns with a brown dress.

Just slip this on for the heck of it.

MILADY exits. JOHANNA puts on the dress.

I think the skirt's a better length for you. This one is more sophisticated with the three-quarter sleeves and fancy belt. And material like that, all it would ever need is a light press. Maybe not even that. Can I take another peek?

JOHANNA: Mm hm.

MILADY opens the curtain and enters. This time JOHANNA doesn't look as if she's been stuck in a garment for a joke.

MILADY: There! It's the colour of your eyes. You don't need to wear velvet. You've got velvet eyes.

JOHANNA: They're just a kind of brown.

MILADY: Now I bet you don't wear dress shoes very often. But if you had nylons on and just a minimum kind of pump— And I bet you don't wear jewellery, and you're quite right, you don't need to with that belt.

JOHANNA: Well, I'd better take it off so you can wrap it up.

MILADY exits as JOHANNA changes.

MILADY: I just hope it's for a special occasion.

JOHANNA: It'll likely be what I get married in.

JOHANNA is surprised at that information coming out of her mouth.

MILADY: Oh! Oh, that's wonderful.

JOHANNA hands the dress to MILADY and begins to put on her old dress.

MILADY: I'll wrap it in tissue paper, all you have to do is take
                 it out and hang it up and the material will fall out
                 beautifully. Just give it a light press if you want, but
                 you probably won't even need to do that.

JOHANNA: Fine.

                 *MILADY gets tissue paper, ribbon, scissors and a big
                 pink box ready at the cash desk.*

MILADY: *(While packing up the dress.)* Where did you meet
                 him? What was your first date?

JOHANNA: Through family. The Western Fair. In London.

MILADY: The Western Fair. In London.

JOHANNA: We had his daughter and her friend with us. They
                 had *me* with *them*.

MILADY: Some days I think how grand it would be, to be
                 married and stay at home. Of course, I used to be
                 married, and I worked anyway. Ah, well. Maybe the
                 man in the moon will walk in here and fall in love
                 with me and then I'll be all set!

                 JOHANNA peels off some bills.

MILADY: It's worth the price. You only get married the once.
                 Well, that's not always strictly true—

JOHANNA: In my case, it'll be true.

                 *JOHANNA hands over the money and exits with the
                 big pink gift box.*

MILADY: All the best.

Scene 3

                 McCAULEY house. JOHANNA enters.

JOHANNA: Hello? Mr. McCauley?

There is no answer. She goes back for the big pink box and re-enters. The phone rings. JOHANNA hides the box in a closet and picks up the phone.

McCauley residence. Yes, this is Johanna Parry speaking. Oh, thank you for calling me back. I want to transfer money from my account. Yes, I have it right here.

SHE takes bank book from purse and refers to it.

It's 5224. I'll come by tomorrow morning. No, it has to be tomorrow. I'll come by first thing. Good-bye.

JOHANNA hangs up the phone, takes the box from the closet and exits.

Scene 4

Train station. STATION AGENT is in the middle of a conversation with MR. McCAULEY.

STATION AGENT: I know everybody in town.

McCAULEY: Her name is Johanna Parry.

STATION AGENT: Well, the core people. The ones who are really in town.

McCAULEY: She said she was leaving on a train today.

STATION AGENT: Johanna Parry. Was she old or young-looking? Thin? Moderately heavy? What was she wearing?

McCAULEY: How would I know?

STATION AGENT: There must me something you can tell me about her.

McCAULEY: She had a load of furniture with her.

STATION AGENT: Furniture? Oh, I know who you mean now. That's your housekeeper?

McCAULEY: Yes.

STATION AGENT: I thought she was maybe a farm woman; with those shoes, and ankle socks instead of stockings, and no hat or gloves in the afternoon. But she didn't have country manners—in fact, she had no manners at all. She treated me like an information machine.

She arranged for her ticket and shipping three days ago.

McCAULEY: Three days ago!

STATION AGENT: Left on the nine-eighteen mixed train this morning.

McCAULEY: She had no right to that furniture. It belonged to my daughter; my daughter who died.

STATION AGENT: That's terrible. Well, Mr. McCauley, if I'd known what she was up to, I never would have let her set foot on that train with your property.

McCAULEY: She had no right to that furniture.

Exiting.

It belonged to my daughter.

STATION AGENT: I'd never have let her set foot on that train if I'd known she'd stolen that furniture! I never would have let her on that train.

Lights down.

Scene 5

Hotel restaurant. MR. McCAULEY enters and sits. WAITRESS enters with a menu.

WAITRESS: Mr. McCauley! You're bright and early today. Don't usually see you 'til lunch.

McCAULEY: My housekeeper walked out on me.

WAITRESS: Sorry to hear that, sir.

McCAULEY: Without any warning or provocation. Took a load of furniture while she was at it. Took a train.

              He waves a letter.

WAITRESS: She took all the furniture out of your house?

McCAULEY: No, it was in the barn behind the house. It was bought with my daughter's wedding money. My daughter, Marcelle.

WAITRESS: Why would she take your daughter's furniture?

McCAULEY: That Ken Boudreau was in on it with her. My son-in-law. Marcelle ran off with him.

WAITRESS: Your housekeeper and your daughter? With the same man?

McCAULEY: No. No. Marcelle is dead.

WAITRESS: I'm sorry for your loss.

McCAULEY: It was years ago now. I suppose he thinks the furniture belongs to him now since it was a wedding present but it doesn't really. It's Sabitha's.

WAITRESS: Who's Sabitha?

McCAULEY: His daughter. My granddaughter.

WAITRESS: Oh.

McCAULEY: The thing that galls me is that on the very day that Johanna bought that train ticket, I got this letter from Boudreau, asking me to "A", advance some money against the furniture or "B", sell it for as much as I can get and send it to Saskatchewan. I sent him some money too; making sure he knew it was a loan; that he had to pay me back. But I put a stop payment on it this morning as soon as I found out what they were up to.

WAITRESS: Good for you.

McCAULEY: Found a letter from her too. Saying she'll waive her three weeks' pay. I have a mind to prosecute them both. Left me some beef stew in a double boiler. I don't how to use a double boiler.

WAITRESS: Excuse me. I'd love to chat, but I've got people waiting on their breakfast. Excuse me—

> *She exits. McCAULEY sits for a moment. He puts money on the table and exits. WAITRESS returns with cutlery. She sees that he has gone. She pockets the money.*

Poor old guy.

> *She exits.*

Scene 6

> *Shultz Shoe Repair Shop. EDITH is working at the counter. Bell rings as the door opens. MR. McCAULEY enters.*

McCAULEY: Good morning.

EDITH: Morning. Are you picking up?

McCAULEY: What? No. You're through school?

EDITH: It's Saturday.

McCAULEY: Well, it's a good thing to help your father, anyway. You must take care of your parents. They've worked hard and they're good people.

EDITH: Papa!

> *HERMAN enters.*

HERMAN: What is it, Edith? Oh, good morning Mr. McCauley.

McCAULEY: Herman.

HERMAN: How can I help you?

EDITH retreats to the shelves.

McCAULEY: Do you remember those boots you resoled for me, the ones I got in England? You resoled them four or five years ago.

HERMAN: Yes, I do. They were nice boots. Do they need to be looked at again?

McCAULEY: No, no, no. They're fine boots. Fine boots. You know I got them on my wedding trip in England.

HERMAN: I remember you telling me.

McCAULEY: You did a fine job on them. Fine job, Herman. You do a good job here. You do honest work.

HERMAN: That's good.

HERMAN picks up a tool.

McCAULEY: I've just had an eye-opener. A shock.

McCAULEY takes the letter from his pocket and begins to refer to it.

HERMAN: What's that, Mr. McCauley?

McCAULEY: A letter from Ken Boudreau. Sabitha's father. Says he doesn't know where to turn to. Bronchitis. Says he's sick with bronchitis. When he's run through everything else, turn to me. "A few hundred just till I get on my feet." Begging and pleading with me and all the time he's conniving with my housekeeper. Did you know that? She stole a load of furniture and went off out west with it.

EDITH drops a shoe.

EDITH: Sorry.

McCAULEY: He could always get around women. This is a man I've saved the skin of, time and time again. And never a penny back. Those Air Force fellows; always strutting around thinking they were war heroes. Well, I guess I shouldn't say that, but I think the war spoiled some of those fellows, they never could adjust to life afterwards. But that's not enough of an excuse. Is it? I can't excuse him forever because of the war.

HERMAN: No you can't.

McCAULEY: At least they did this after Sabitha left. Her Aunt Roxanne has her down in Toronto now. Of course you both know that. I'm taking up your time, I'm imposing on you. You have work to do. Good-bye, Herman.

MR. McCAULEY exits.

HERMAN: Good-bye. *(To EDITH.)* He's not himself. I'd have thought he'd be the last person to go on like that. But here he is with some letter… Something's come over him.

HERMAN exits.

The lights have gradually dimmed on HERMAN as EDITH has come into sharper focus.

Lights up on JOHANNA carrying her coat and wearing her new dress. She is on a train station platform in Gdynia, Saskatchewan. We hear the sound of a receding train. EDITH watches her.

JOHANNA: Hello. Hello? Anybody here?

JOHANNA looks about, picks up her suitcase and sets out.

Act One

Scene 1

      Shultz kitchen. SABITHA enters.

SABITHA: *(Taking it all in.)* Huh!

EDITH: *(From off.)* Abitha-Say?

SABITHA: What? Oh. Turn.

EDITH: *(From off.)* Ardon-pay e-may Abitha-say? *[Pardon me, Sabitha?]*

SABITHA: I mean…uh…urn-tay. *[turn]*

EDITH: *(From off.)* Ank-they ou-yay. At-way ext-nay? *[Thank you. What next?]*

SABITHA: Oh, uh… Evven-say eps-stay.

      [Seven steps.]

EDITH: Evven-say.

      SABITHA looks around.

SABITHA: Jeepers, it's dark in here.

EDITH: *(From off.)* ABITHA-SAY?!

SABITHA: Just a second, Edith. Now. I mean, ow-nay *[now]*. Aight-stray *[straight]*… *(This is a difficult one.)* Ahead-*ay*?

      EDITH enters, blindfolded. Her hair and clothing are slightly different from when she was in the shoe repair shop. She is carrying an armload of school books.

EDITH:	Ahead-*yay*. Use a 'y' in front of a vowel.
SABITHA:	Ahead-yay.
EDITH:	Ere-way oo-day I-yay ut-pay eye-may ooks-bay? *[Where do I put my books?]*
SABITHA:	Ere-hay *[Here]*. Urn-tay ight-ray *[Turn right]*— (EDITH *turns right*) Urn-tay eft-lay! *[Turn left!]* (EDITH *does*). Alk-way un-way ep-stay. *[Walk one step]*

> EDITH *steps toward the table.* EDITH *bumps into it and knows where she is.*

EDITH:	(*Putting down her books and taking off blindfold. She sits at the table.*) Ell-way un-day, owly-lay urm-way.
SABITHA:	Ell-way... Well un—Well done...?
EDITH:	Well done, lowly worm.
SABITHA:	Thanks a bunch.
EDITH:	Do you want some tea?
SABITHA:	Don't you have any fizzy drinks?
EDITH:	(*Checking even though she knows there isn't any.*) We must be out.
SABITHA:	OK. Tea, then. With lots of milk and sugar.

> EDITH *fills the kettle and puts it on the stove while* SABITHA *wanders around, checking things out.*

SABITHA:	You're so lucky your parents are at work all day. I'd love to have my house to myself. Wanna watch television?
EDITH:	Maybe later.

> EDITH *picks up a math textbook and a notebook and starts working.*

SABITHA:	You're doing your homework now?
EDITH:	It won't take long. It should be easy for you. You did it all last year.
SABITHA:	Yeah, I was perfect in all my classes. That's why I got left back. Let's play one more game. I know a good one.
EDITH:	My mom likes me to do my homework before dinner. She always checks it.
SABITHA:	Granddad couldn't be bothered. And Johanna wouldn't understand it anyway.
EDITH:	I guess you're the lucky one.
SABITHA:	Come on.

She takes a piece of paper from EDITH's work.

EDITH:	Hey!
SABITHA:	First I write down my name. Then I write down the name of a boy that I like.
EDITH:	Colin Jansen.
SABITHA:	He's so dreamy. I write down both our names, then I cross out all the letters we have in common. After that, I use the letters that are left over.

SABITHA writes.

SABITHA:	I say a different word for each letter left over. Hateship, Friendship, Courtship, Loveship, Marriage.
EDITH:	Then what?
SABITHA:	It's easier if I just do it.

SABITHA ticks off the letters with the pen.

Hateship, Friendship, Courtship, Loveship,

Marriage. Hateship, Friendship, Courtship, Loveship, Marriage. Hateship, Friendship, Courtship, *Loveship.* (*Squeals with delight.*) Me and Colin Jansen are going to fall in love! I told you it was fun. Let's find a boy for you.

EDITH: In a minute.

EDITH works from her textbook.

SABITHA: Can't have any fun with you.

SABITHA picks up her books and begins to leave.

EDITH: You're leaving?

SABITHA: Well, if you're going to be so boring.

EDITH: OK. Look. I'm closing my books. See?

SABITHA: Have I got the perfect boy for you! Oh no. I forgot to mail my letter to my dad.

The kettle whistles. EDITH turns off the burner as SABITHA plays the game.

Edith Shultz and... (*SABITHA mutters words and letters.*)

EDITH: Did you have a lot to write to your dad?

SABITHA: I only wrote one page.

SABITHA continues with the game. EDITH's eye is still drawn to the letter.

EDITH: It's a fat letter for only one page.

EDITH is examining the letter, feeling the weight; holding it up to the light.

A-ha. Ah. Ha.

SABITHA: Aha what?

The kettle whistles. SABITHA is ready to pour the

> *hot water but EDITH holds the envelope over the spout.*

> What are you doing?

EDITH: You'll see.

SABITHA: How often do you do this?

EDITH: I admit nothing.

> *EDITH removes two letters.*

> Ah ha!

SABITHA: *(Indicating one of the letters.)* I didn't write that one.

EDITH: Johanna did.

SABITHA: Johanna?

EDITH: How did she get her letter in with yours without you knowing?

SABITHA: She just takes it from me and puts it in an envelope and writes the address. She doesn't think my writing is good enough.

EDITH: *(Reading.)* "Dear Mr. Boudreau. I just thought I would write and send my thanks to you for the nice things you said about me in your letter to your daughter."

SABITHA: What!?

EDITH: What did he say about her?

SABITHA: He said she was a lady. He said he could tell. And how it would be too bad if she left because Granddad couldn't raise a girl by himself and blah-blah.

EDITH: "You do not need to worry about me leaving."

SABITHA: Lucky me.

EDITH: "You say that I am a person you can trust. I am grateful to you for saying that since some people feel that a person they do not know the background of is Beyond the Pale. So I thought I would tell you something about myself."

SABITHA: Why bother?

EDITH: "I was born in Glasgow, but my mother had to give me up when she got married."

SABITHA: What?!

                This bit of juicy information changes everything. The letter is now very interesting as both girls move in to examine it more clearly. Lights change as JOHANNA begins to read the letter.

JOHANNA: I was taken to the Home at the age of five. I looked for her to come back, but she didn't and I got used to it there and they weren't Bad.

                At the age of eleven I was brought to Canada on a Plan and lived with the Dixons, working on their Market Gardens. School was in the Plan, but I didn't see much of it. In winter I worked in the house for the Mrs. but circumstances made me think of leaving and being big and strong for my age got taken on at a Nursing Home looking after the old people. I did not mind the work, but for better money went and worked in a Broom Factory. Mr. Willets who owned it had an old mother that came in to see how things were going and she and I took to each other in some way so she said I should come and work for her and I did. I lived with her twelve years on a lake called Mourning Dove Lake up north. There was only the two of us, but I could take care of everything outside and in, even running the motorboat and driving the car. I learned to read properly because her eyes were going bad and she liked me to read to her. She died at the age of 96.

You might say what a life for a young person, but I was happy. After she died, her family gave me one week to pack up. She had left me some money and I guess they did not like that. So when I saw the ad Mr. McCauley put in the Globe and Mail I came to see about it. I needed work to get over missing Mrs. Willets.

So I guess I have bored you long enough with my History and you'll be relieved I have got up to the Present. Thank you for your good opinion and for taking me along to the Fair.

Your friend,

JOHANNA/
EDITH: Johanna Parry.

                Lights down on JOHANNA.

EDITH: I was born in Glasgow, but my mother had to give me up when she took one look at me—

SABITHA: *(Laughing.)* Stop. I'm going to be sick.

EDITH: I bet she flew to that Broom Factory every day.

SABITHA: She's pathetic.

EDITH: She's in love with him.

SABITHA: Oh, puke-puke.

                EDITH folds the letter and starts putting it back into the envelope.

EDITH: She's in love with your dad.

SABITHA: She can't be. Old Johanna.

EDITH: *(Re-sealing the envelope and handing her the letter.)* Go mail it. Then we'll see what he writes back.

                SABITHA exits.

Scene 2

Lights up on Shultz kitchen. SABITHA and EDITH drink fizzy drinks.

EDITH: Brussels!

SABITHA: Really? You can ride your bike there.

EDITH: The one in Belgium.

SABITHA: Oh.

EDITH: Your turn.

SABITHA: Career?

EDITH nods.

Secretary.

EDITH: You can't even type.

SABITHA: I won't have to. My rich and handsome boss will fall in love with me on my first day. We'll get married and I'll never have to work again. Secretary.

EDITH: Yangtze River!

SABITHA: Hm. Receptionist!

EDITH: So you can marry a rich and handsome boss.

SABITHA: Who will fall in love with me on the first day.

EDITH: It's too much like secretary.

SABITHA: Nothing starts with R.

EDITH: How about Rodeo Clown?

SABITHA: Fine. I like cowboys.

EDITH: Nobel Prize winner in science…and literature … and peace.

SABITHA: OK, so what's my letter?

EDITH: Nobel Prize *Winner.*

SABITHA: Regina.

EDITH: Regina?

SABITHA: That's where Colin's from.

EDITH: Art Dealer.

SABITHA: That's another R.

EDITH: OK. Artist.

SABITHA: Typist.

EDITH: Sabitha!

SABITHA: What?

EDITH: Never mind.

SABITHA: Let's play the Hateship game.

EDITH: But aren't you and Colin in "loveship?"

EDITH: Loveship's not a word, by the way.

SABITHA: Well, it should be.

EDITH: Neither's hateship.

SABITHA: You're so mean. I was going to show you the letter my dad wrote to me but now—

EDITH: Your dad finally wrote back?

SABITHA shows her a letter.

SABITHA: I steamed it open.

SABITHA displays the envelope on the table.

EDITH: Well done, lowly worm. It took him long enough.

SABITHA: That's my dad.

EDITH: Just one letter.

SABITHA: Yep.

EDITH: "Dear Sabitha, Christmas finds me a bit short this year, sorry I don't have more than a two-dollar bill to send you."

> *SABITHA shows her the money.*

"I hope you are in good health and have a Merry Christmas and keep up your schoolwork. I have not been feeling so well myself, having got Bronchitis, which I seem to do every winter. As you see by the address I am in a new place. The apartment was in a very noisy location and too many people dropping in hoping for a party. This is a boarding house, which suits me fine as I was never good at the shopping and the cooking.

Merry Christmas and love..."

EDITH: "Dad." No. Nothing. Poor Johanna. Her heart will be *bwoken.*

SABITHA: Who cares?

EDITH: Unless we do it.

SABITHA: What?

EDITH: Answer her.

> *EDITH is gone in a flash, returning with a typewriter that she sets up on the table.*

SABITHA: "Dear Johanna, I am sorry I cannot be in love with you because you have got those ugly spots all over your face."

EDITH: I'm going to be serious. So shut up.

> *The paper is set up in the typewriter and EDITH types.*

"Dear Johanna."

She takes a moment to think.

"I was so glad to get the letter—"

SABITHA: Blah-blah...blah blah, blah blah.

EDITH: "...and to find out about your life." Good start.

SABITHA: Blah blah blah blah blah—

EDITH: Pul-eeze. How can I concentrate on my emotions with all that *shit* going on?

They revel in saying the forbidden words.

SABITHA: You don't have to be a *bitch* about it.

EDITH: Just give me five minutes for *shit's* sake.

SABITHA: You can't write a letter in five *shit* minutes.

EDITH: *Shit,* just watch me.

SABITHA: *Shit,* alright.

EDITH: Thank you.

EDITH types.

SABITHA: You're so fast.

EDITH continues to type.

You could be a secretary.

EDITH: *(Still typing.)* Bite your tongue.

SABITHA tries to see what EDITH is writing. EDITH elbows her out of the way. SABITHA gets a piece of paper and a pen.

SABITHA: Edith Shultz. Is there a "C" in Shultz?

EDITH: No.

SABITHA: Edith Shultz and Victor Ferguson. *(Writing.)* Hateship, Friendship, Courtship...

EDITH: Shut up.

SABITHA: Alright. Alright.

> *SABITHA continues with the game speaking the words ('Hateship, Friendship, Courtship') softly. EDITH continues to type. Unable to contain her excitement, SABITHA shouts out her results.*

SABITHA: Courtship! Victor Ferguson is going to court you.

EDITH: He can try.

> *EDITH stops typing.*

SABITHA: Are you done?

EDITH: Just coming up with the perfect ending. Ah ha!

> *EDITH finishes typing and takes the page from the typewriter. She hands it to SABITHA.*

EDITH: I tried to show that they are kindred spirits.

SABITHA: Yeah. Yeah. "Dear Johanna. I was so glad to get the letter you put in with Sabitha's and to find out about your life.

> *Lights up on JOHANNA.*

SABITHA: "It must often have been a sad and lonely one...

> *Lights fade on EDITH and SABITHA.*

JOHANNA: "...though Mrs. Willets sounds like a lucky person for you to find. You have remained industrious and uncomplaining and I must say that I admire you very much. My own life has been a checkered one and I have never exactly settled down. I do not know why I have this inner restlessness and loneliness, it just seems to be my fate. Sometimes I ask myself, Who is my friend? Then comes your letter and you write at the end of it, Your friend. So I think, Does she really mean that? And what a very nice Christmas present it would be for me if Johanna would tell me that she is my friend. Maybe you just thought it was a nice way to end a letter and you don't really know me well enough. Merry Christmas anyway.

Lights up on the girls.

SABITHA/
JOHANNA: Your friend, Ken Boudreau."

Lights down on JOHANNA.

EDITH: Well?

SABITHA: It's just like if he wrote it. How did you do that?

EDITH: *(Quite pleased with herself.)* Now I have to type the letter he wrote to you.

                EDITH puts a new sheet of paper in the typewriter.

SABITHA: Why?

EDITH: Why would one letter be typed and not the other?

SABITHA: Why couldn't we type a new envelope?

EDITH: Because a new *envelope* wouldn't have a *postmark* on it. Dumb-dumb.

SABITHA: What if she answers it?

EDITH: We'll read it.

SABITHA: Yeah, what if she answers it and sends it direct to *him*?

EDITH: *(Not wanting to show that she hadn't thought of this.)* She won't. She's sly. Anyway, you write him back right away to give her the idea she can slip it in with yours again.

SABITHA: I hate writing stupid letters.

EDITH: Don't you want to see what she says?

                SABITHA begins to write the letter.

EDITH: "Dear Sabitha. Christmas finds me a bit short this
                year…"

                EDITH types as lights fade.

Scene 3

                *McCauley house. JOHANNA reads the letter. When
                she's done, she gets out a pen and writing tablet. She
                begins to write back.*

JOHANNA: *(Writing.)* Dear Friend, you ask me do I know you
                well enough to be your friend and my answer is
                that I think I do.

                Lights down.

Scene 4

                *Shultz kitchen. Lights up to reveal EDITH and
                SABITHA huddled over a letter.*

EDITH: *(Reading.)* "I have had only one Friend in my life,
                Mrs. Willets who I loved and she was so good to me
                but she is dead.

                *SABITHA moves to the fridge and starts checking
                out the contents, even sampling from jars.*

                I will tell you a strange thing. That picture that
                you got the photographer at the Fair to take of
                you and Sabitha and her friend Edith and me, I
                had it enlarged and framed and set in the living
                room. It is not a very good picture and he certainly
                charged you enough for what it is, but it is better
                than nothing. So the day before yesterday I was

dusting around it and I imagined I could hear you say Hello to me."

SABITHA: *(Rushing over from the fridge.)* You're making that up.

EDITH: *(Showing her the passage in the letter.)* "Hello, you said, and I looked at your face as well as you can see it in the picture and I thought, Well I must be losing my mind."

SABITHA: Absolutely.

EDITH: "Or else it's a sign of a letter coming. I am just fooling, I don't really believe in anything like that. But yesterday there was a letter. So you see it is not asking too much of me to be your friend. I can always find a way to keep busy but a true Friend is something else again. Your Friend, Johanna Parry."

SABITHA: She's insane.

EDITH: She's in love. Johanna's gonna be your stepmother!

SABITHA: Shut up.

EDITH: You'll have to call her Mommy. She'll make you wear old lady shoes and dresses from pioneer days. You'll look like twins.

SABITHA: I said shut up. Shut up, you stupid bitch!

EDITH does.

SABITHA: I don't have to be friends with you, you know.

EDITH: I know.

EDITH rips up the letter.

SABITHA: What did you do that for?

EDITH: She wrote about things from a letter your father never wrote. He'd spot something fishy.

SABITHA: You're a regular Nancy Drew.

EDITH: Thank you.

SABITHA: Should we write her another letter?

EDITH: Oh, that would be swell but we need his letter so the envelope has the postmark.

SABITHA: Right. Well, knowing my dad that won't be 'til summer. I can't wait. So sick of winter.

EDITH: Me too.

> *Things seem back to normal. Hurt feelings have been cast aside.*

SABITHA: What are you doing this summer?

EDITH: Working in my parents' shop. Full time.

SABITHA: Ew. Stuck with smelly shoes.

EDITH: It's not that bad.

SABITHA: I'll be up at the cottage.

EDITH: I didn't know you had a cottage.

SABITHA: It belongs to my Aunt Roxanne and Uncle Clark from Toronto. We're going for three weeks! Too bad you can't come.

EDITH: Yeah. Will you flush away the incriminating evidence?

SABITHA: With the greatest of pleasure.

> *SABITHA exits. EDITH seems exhausted at the work she just put into saving the friendship. A toilet flushes.*

EDITH: (*Calling.*) Well done, lowly worm!

> *SABITHA giggles offstage.*

Scene 5

McCauley house. JOHANNA is mopping the floor. MR. McCAULEY enters. He is reading the newspaper, holding it very far from his face, and walks toward the wet section of the floor.

JOHANNA: Sir—

He walks obliviously over the clean spot.

McCAULEY: Yes?

JOHANNA: Nothing. Did you need something?

He searches his pockets. He wants to say he can't find his glasses but can't bring himself to.

McCAULEY: What time's dinner?

JOHANNA: Six o'clock. Chicken and biscuits.

He grunts an acknowledgement and exits. After a moment, He returns.

McCAULEY: Johanna, have you seen my glasses?

JOHANNA: They're on the kitchen counter, sir.

McCAULEY: Thank you.

He exits. JOHANNA resumes mopping.

Scene 6

Shultz kitchen. SABITHA knocks and enters. She is wearing a sun suit.

EDITH: Welcome back.

SABITHA: Ugga-ugga. This place stinks. I got us some éclairs. Do you have any coffee?

EDITH: Instant.

SABITHA: Instant will do. All we drank at the cottage was iced coffee.

EDITH: I've already put the kettle on.

            She takes two coffee mugs from the cupboard.

SABITHA: No. Not those.

            SABITHA searches through the cupboard and removes two tall glasses.

SABITHA: That's more like it. Ice please. Ugga-ugga. This place does stink.

            EDITH gets the ice tray from the freezer. SABITHA puts the ice cubes in the glasses.

EDITH: I don't smell anything.

SABITHA: It's like your dad's shop, only not so bad. What was even better was iced coffee with vanilla ice cream. Oh, my Gad, is it ever wonderful. Do you have vanilla ice cream?

EDITH: No.

SABITHA: It'll still be good.

            Kettle whistles.

SABITHA: Look what I found at the post office!

EDITH: Jeepers, I'd all but given up.

SABITHA: Don't you like my outfit?

EDITH: Is it supposed to be that short?

SABITHA: Oh, Edith.

EDITH: Oh, Edith—What?

SABITHA: I'd just forgotten what you're like.

EDITH: You were only away for three weeks.

SABITHA: Three very short weeks. Don't you want your éclair?

EDITH: Yes. All of it. *(She has finished steaming open the letter.)* Just one letter. For you. *Pore* old Johanna. Of course he never actually *got* hers.

            EDITH gives the letter to SABITHA.

SABITHA: *(Reads.)* "Well, Sabitha, my fortunes have taken a different turn, as you can see I am not in Brandon anymore but in a place called Gdynia. And not in the employ of my former bosses. I have had an exceptionally hard winter with my chest troubles. Blah blah.

            SABITHA puts down the letter and returns to her éclair.

EDITH: Don't stop.

SABITHA: You read it. I've got sticky guck all over my hands.

            EDITH takes the letter.

EDITH: *(Finding her place.)* "But luck is a strange thing and I just came into possession of a hotel. If your grandfather wants to know about it just tell him a man who owed me money which he could not pay let me have this hotel instead. So here I am moved from one room in a boarding house to a twelve-bedroom building and from not even owning the bed I slept in to owning several. It's a wonderful thing to wake up in the morning and know you are your own boss. I have some fixing up to do, actually plenty, and will get to it as soon as the weather warms up. Hope you are well and doing your schoolwork and developing good habits.

            Love, Your Dad."

            SABITHA has finished making the iced coffees and gives EDITH a glass of it.

SABITHA: Here.

They toast and take a sip. It is delicious.

You haven't said anything about my hair.

EDITH: It's nice.

SABITHA: My cousins cut it and gave me a permanent. You should get one too. My cousins know all the latest fashions. I learned so much from them. And not just about hair and clothes. We older girls slept upstairs in the boathouse. Sometimes we would have tickling fights. We would gang up on one of the girls; you know, one of the younger ones and tickle her. We'd only stop if she pulled her pyjama pants down, to show if she had *hair*.

They told stories about girls at their private school who did things with hairbrush handles.

Ugga-ugga. My Uncle Clark's sister and her husband came to visit on their honeymoon and we saw him put his hand inside her swimsuit.

EDITH: Out in public?

SABITHA: Right on the dock. They were at it day and night. They really loved each other. And...one of my cousins *did it* with a boy. He worked at the resort and took her out in a boat. He said he'd push her out if she didn't let him so it wasn't her fault.

EDITH: Couldn't she swim?

SABITHA: And guess who's moving to Toronto!

EDITH: When?

SABITHA: Soon! After Aunt Roxanne dropped me off today, I heard her tell Granddad that he and Johanna wouldn't be able to handle me when the boys "come swarming around." Isn't that great?

EDITH: It means that they don't trust you.

SABITHA: Who cares? I'm moving to Toronto.

SABITHA starts playing with a cushion.

EDITH: *(About the iced coffee.)* Needs more sugar.

She goes to the counter.

SABITHA: Oooh.

EDITH: *(Sees what SABITHA's doing.)* Sabitha!

SABITHA: Feels so nice.

EDITH: *(Looking around to make sure no one else is around.)* Stop!

SABITHA: It's nothing. We all did it like this.

EDITH looks away.

Oooh.

EDITH grabs the cushion away and flings it to the floor.

EDITH: You could get into trouble doing that. My mother told me!

SABITHA: Didn't you know I was kidding?

EDITH says nothing.

SABITHA: Can't have any fun with you.

EDITH picks up the letter.

SABITHA: Are we going to write Johanna another letter? "My darlingest Johanna..."

EDITH: No. That's too sickening.

SABITHA: "Your last letter filled me with rap-ture..."

EDITH: "Your last letter made me so happy to think I did have a true friend in the world, which is you."

SABITHA:	"I couldn't sleep all night because I was longing to crush you in my arms…"
EDITH:	*No.* "Often I have felt so lonely in spite of a gregarious life and not known where to turn."
SABITHA:	What does that mean—'gregarious'? She won't know what it means.
EDITH:	*She* will.

EDITH gets the typewriter. SABITHA sulks.

EDITH:	"I imagine you reading this and blushing." Is that more what you want?
SABITHA:	"Reading it in bed with your nightgown on and thinking how I would crush you in my arms and I would suck your titties."
EDITH:	The nightgown part is good.

EDITH begins to type. Lights fade on girls and come up on JOHANNA.

JOHANNA:	"When I was feverish I had a dream. I dreamt that I saw your dear sweet face bending over me and I heard your voice telling me I would soon be better and I felt the ministrations of your kind hands. I was in the boarding house and when I came to out of my fever there was a lot of teasing going on as to, who is this Johanna? But I was sad as could be to wake and to find you were not there.
	I don't know if I should tell you the other things you were saying to me in my dream because they were very sweet and intimate but they might embarrass you. I hate to end this letter because it feels now as if I have my arms around you and am talking to you quietly in the dark privacy of our room, but I must say good-bye and the only way I can do it is to imagine you reading this and blushing. It would be wonderful if you were reading it in bed with

your nightgown on and thinking how I would like
to crush you in my arms.

Love, Ken Boudreau."

> *Lights down on JOHANNA. Lights up on SABITHA
> and EDITH. EDITH takes the page from the
> typewriter.*

SABITHA: Not bad. Not bad at all.

> *Lights down.*

Scene 7

> *McCauley house. MR. McCAULEY is reading the
> newspaper at arm's length. He searches through his
> pockets for his glasses. He can't find them.*

McCAULEY: Johanna? Johanna?

> *He exits.*

(l to r): Catherine Fitch (Johanna) and Gil Garratt (Ken)

Act Two

Scene 1

Dishevelled Gdynia hotel bedroom. KEN is asleep in a messy bed. From far off, we hear JOHANNA's voice.

JOHANNA: *(From off.)* Hello. *(Footsteps approach the door.)* Hello. *(There is a tap on the door.)* Hello?

> *JOHANNA enters. She is wearing her new dress and carries her coat, suitcase and purse.*

Good morning. Afternoon.

> *KEN emits a few coughs.*

Ken?

> *HE coughs again and faces her.*

KEN: Who are you?

JOHANNA: It's me, Johanna.

> *HE coughs violently, drowning out her answer and struggles to sit up. JOHANNA goes to the bed and hoists him up. She looks around for something and settles for a shirt on the floor. She holds it to his mouth. KEN hacks into the shirt. He sinks back down, exhausted.*
>
> *JOHANNA checks his temperature then examines the phlegm.*

How long have you been sick? Ken?

She covers him with stray clothing and exits with the shirt to the sink (offstage). KEN's laboured breathing and wheezing underscores the scene. The water runs as JOHANNA washes the shirt, then re-enters, hanging it on the back of the bedside chair. She takes the clothes piled on the chair and throws them on the floor. She exits to wash her hands and re-enters. She looks for something with which to dry her hands. Finding nothing, she dries them thoroughly on the skirt of her new dress.

She helps KEN get into a better position in bed.

Come on.

She covers him again. JOHANNA removes the overflowing ashtray from the chair and takes it to the bathroom. The toilet flushes. JOHANNA returns with the empty ashtray and raises the stiff window an inch or two, propping it open with the ashtray. She removes the curtains and places them on one of the piles of clothing before hanging up her coat on a hook and setting down her purse. She clears dishes and a whisky bottle from the floor and headboard. Exits.

KEN throws the covers off himself, sits up and looks around.

KEN: Hello?

He goes back to sleep.

Scene 2

JOHANNA enters with a basket filled with bedding. She has changed back into her shapeless dress. She tries to turn on the lamp on the headboard but it doesn't work. She notices a set of keys and puts them aside. She covers KEN with a blanket. She exits to the bathroom and returns with a glass of water. She rests it on the headboard. He begins to cough and she helps him sit up while she holds toilet paper to his mouth and pounds his back. He stops coughing and she settles him back into bed. She examines the toilet paper while he falls asleep. JOHANNA exits with the tissue and cloth. The toilet flushes. She washes her hands and re-enters, drying her hands on one of the towels.

JOHANNA raises KEN to a sitting position.

JOHANNA: Come on. That's it.

She sits on the chair and tries to get him to drink.

Here.

After a few sips, he coughs. She tries to get him to drink some more.

KEN: No!

He knocks the glass out of her hands.

No.

He flops down on the bed. She picks up the glass and exits, gets some more water from the tap, returns with a full glass, sits and holds it to his mouth again.

JOHANNA: Come on. You have to drink some water. Come on.

He drinks, then falls asleep on her shoulder. JOHANNA lets him rest for a moment.

A little bit more.

She helps him drink more water.

	Lights down.
Scene 3	

Lights up on KEN. The lamp is now on. There are fewer clothes strewn around the room. JOHANNA enters with sheets. She changes the sheets, rolling KEN to one side and removing the dirty ones as she goes along.

KEN: *(Sitting up, delirious.)* I could really use a drink. How about you?

JOHANNA keeps working.

JOHANNA: Lie down, Ken.

KEN: Let's go for a drink.

JOHANNA: *(Not breaking stride.)* Just lie down, Ken.

KEN: Yep.

He lies down. She continues making the bed. She begins to roll him over.

Not across the border.

JOHANNA: Alright.

KEN: Not across the border.

JOHANNA: I won't.

KEN: No way.

JOHANNA: Nope.

KEN: You tell that sergeant it was a joke.

JOHANNA: OK.

She covers him with the blanket.

KEN: You tell him it was just a joke.

JOHANNA: I'll tell him. It was a good one.

KEN: Tell him I quit.

JOHANNA: Alright.

              *She tidies a bit and exits with the dirty sheets. KEN
              has settled down*

              Lights down.

Scene 4

              *There is even less clothing on the floor. KEN is sitting
              up. JOHANNA sits on the chair and feeds him soup.
              He is quite weak and takes little sips. This is the
              most awake he has been. The sound of the washing
              machine fades out. KEN coughs. JOHANNA checks
              his temperature.*

JOHANNA: Do you have a bottle of aspirin?

              KEN nods.

              Where?

KEN: In the wastebasket.

JOHANNA: No, no. You don't mean wastebasket.

KEN: In the—in the—

              *He tries to shape something with his hands. His
              frustration leads him to tears. He lies down.*

JOHANNA: Never mind. Never mind. I'll find it.

              He falls asleep.

              Lights down.

Scene 5

> KEN *is asleep and shirtless.* JOHANNA, *using a cloth which She dips into a basin of water, wipes down his arm and covers him with the blanket. Then, she folds back the blanket and wipes down his chest.*
>
> *Lights down.*

Scene 6

> JOHANNA *drags in an armchair. She places a shirt on the headboard. There are curtains resting on the armchair. She stands on the chair and hangs the curtains at the window. She steps down from the chair and picks up the shirt. She is about to move to* KEN *with it but decides to let him sleep. She re-folds the shirt and places it on the headboard and adjusts the blanket.* JOHANNA *settles into the chair for the night, covering herself with her coat.*
>
> *Lights down.*

Scene 7

> *Lights up. The next morning.* KEN *wakes. It appears as though* JOHANNA *has been awake all night.*

JOHANNA: Good morning.

KEN: What are you doing here?

JOHANNA: I brought your furniture. I got here two days ago.

KEN: Furniture?

JOHANNA: It isn't here yet, but it's on its way. You've been very sick. How do you feel now?

KEN: Better.

She hangs up her coat. He begins to cough.
JOHANNA gets toilet paper. The coughing stops
before she can hand it to him.

JOHANNA: You swallowed the phlegm. Don't do that, it's not
             good for you. Here.

             (She hands him toilet paper) You have to spit it
             out. You could get trouble with your kidneys,
             swallowing it.

KEN: I never knew that. Is there any coffee?

JOHANNA: Alright.

             JOHANNA exits. He gets out of bed and has to
             steady himself for a moment on the arm of the chair.
             He looks through her purse and leaves it on the
             floor, carefully taking out her wallet. He reads the
             identification card.

KEN: *(Reading.)* Johanna Parry. Exhibition Road. Johanna
             Parry.

             He searches through her wallet and finds a few
             bills.

             Twenty-seven dollars.

             He returns the money to exactly where he found it.
             Then he removes a bank book. He opens it and flips
             through the pages until he gets to the final entry. It's
             a surprising amount.

             Johanna Parry.

             The kitchen noises have stopped, prompting him to
             return the bank book and get back into bed. First he
             takes a T-shirt which has been laid out for him, puts
             it on, smells it and lies down.

             Lights dim as time passes.

Scene 8

> *Lights up. KEN is in bed. JOHANNA is folding laundry. KEN wakes up.*

KEN: Were you wearing a brown dress?

JOHANNA: *(Relieved.)* Yes I was. When I first got here.

KEN: I thought it was a dream. It was you.

JOHANNA: Like in your other dream?

> *After a moment, KEN coughs. JOHANNA holds toilet paper to his mouth and pounds his back, much to his surprise.*

KEN: Thank you. Could you see if there's any cigarettes downstairs?

> *JOHANNA shakes her head.*

JOHANNA: I'll look. I've got biscuits in the oven.

> *JOHANNA exits.*

Scene 9

> *JOHANNA is asleep in the armchair, covered by her coat. KEN sneaks out of bed. He holds a whisky bottle and speaks to her.*

KEN: You brought my furniture.

I tell people that I won this place in a poker game. Women like the sound of that. The thing is, I took it in payment of a debt. I just can't seem to say no to a friend. Gets me into trouble sometimes.

It'll work as a bar and restaurant. If I can get a good cook. But I gotta have some money.

I just need a small loan to get through the winter. That's where my father-in-law comes in. Believe me, I'd rather try somebody else, but nobody else can spare it as easily.

I know I have other loans with him but I did support Marcelle, even all through her drug problems, and all the running around. And I accepted Sabitha as my kid. Even though I have my doubts.

KEN takes a swig from the bottle.

There's a woman problem in my life right now. Two women, actually. They know about each other. All I get from them is howling and complaining. They say they love me but...they're so angry. I have to admit drink plays a part.

He puts the stopper in the bottle and ambles into bed.

Lights down.

Scene 10

Hotel bedroom. Day time. A container of flowers is on the headboard. KEN is asleep. Car door slams. A car engine sputters to a start and begins to drive away. KEN wakes suddenly.

KEN: My car! That's my car.

He gets out of bed and looks out the window as the car drives off.

Johanna!

He runs to the door then stops, looks around the room and takes it in, especially the flowers. He realizes that everything will be alright. He sits in the chair.

Time passes.

Scene 11

> Bedroom. The bed has been roughly made. The sputtering car drives up. KEN sits in the armchair. He listens to JOHANNA enter the hotel and walk up the stairs. JOHANNA enters.

JOHANNA: This place is a sinkhole for money.

KEN: Well, I don't know about that—

JOHANNA: The town is on its last legs. What should be done is to take out everything that can bring cash and sell it. I don't mean your wedding furniture. I mean things like the pool table and the kitchen range. Then, we ought to sell the building to somebody who'll strip the tin off it for junk. There's always a bit to be made off stuff you'd never think had any value. Then— What was it you had in mind to do before you got hold of the hotel?

KEN: I was planning on going to British Columbia, to Salmon Arm. A friend told me one time I could have a job managing orchards. But the car needed new tires and work done on it before I could take a long trip. Then this hotel fell into my lap.

JOHANNA: Like a ton of bricks. Tires and fixing the car would be a better investment than sinking anything into this place. It would be a good idea to get out there before the snow comes. And ship the furniture by rail again, to make use of it when we get there. We have got all we need to furnish a home.

KEN: It's maybe not all that firm of an offer.

JOHANNA: I know. But it'll be alright.

> KEN has nothing to say to this. He seems embarrassed. Sound of a truck pulling up.

JOHANNA: That must be the furniture now. I'll just check that they're careful with it. *(After a moment.)* Ken.

KEN: Yes, Johanna?

JOHANNA: I know... I understand... It can be hard to say things face to face. I understand that.

KEN: OK.

She exits.

Lights down.

Epilogue

Funeral home. EDITH enters. She contemplates going into the visitation room. She notices the guest book and skims through a few pages. She writes in it and starts for the room. SABITHA enters.

SABITHA: Edith! I was wondering when you'd show up.

EDITH: Hi Sabitha.

SABITHA: I saw your mom and dad inside.

EDITH: I'm sorry about your grandfather.

SABITHA: I know. Well, you know. Thanks.

EDITH: Yeah.

SABITHA: How are you?

EDITH: OK, I guess. You?

SABITHA: I'm dying for a cigarette. Do you have any?

EDITH: No. Sorry.

SABITHA: Too bad.

EDITH: Should I go in?

SABITHA: Why not?

EDITH: Is she in there?

SABITHA: Who?

EDITH: Johanna.

SABITHA: Oh no. They live in Salmon Arm. It's in B.C.

EDITH: Oh. Did your grandfather…talk to you, or, you know, write about…everything that happened back then?

SABITHA: And how! He said he was going to press charges against both of them for theft. But he never did.

EDITH: Everyone in town was talking about Mr. McCauley's stolen furniture.

SABITHA: Must have been the most exciting thing to happen here in years.

EDITH: I kept waiting to…well…get caught. And then, nothing. Nothing happened and I couldn't understand why.

SABITHA: Because nothing ever happens here.

EDITH: It all seems sort of…fantastical. Don't you think?

SABITHA: I guess.

EDITH: Fantastical and dull, all at the same time.

SABITHA: You have to get out of this place, Edith.

EDITH: I am! At least I think so. I haven't officially been accepted to U of T yet.

SABITHA: You'll love Toronto. I'll take you on the subway. Show you all the great stores.

EDITH: They have a baby.

SABITHA: I know. Omar! Where did they ever come up with that name?

EDITH: Doesn't it all seem…I don't know…like, a joke of some kind. Some…inept joke.

SABITHA: I'll say. Old Johanna with a baby.

EDITH: A joke or, I don't know…a warning.

SABITHA: Get away. That's the warning. Take it from me.

EDITH: You know, Sabitha, on the list of all the things I plan to achieve in my life, there's no mention of being responsible for someone named Omar.

SABITHA: Be cool. It's a happy ending! Come keep me company. Someone out there's got to have a cigarette.

EDITH: My parents will wonder where I am.

SABITHA: Same old Edith. What did you write?

EDITH: Just some poem I had to translate in Latin class.

SABITHA: "You must not ask. It is forbidden for us to know what fate has in store for me or for you." I don't get it.

EDITH: Try the guy at the hardware store. He smokes like a chimney.

SABITHA: Thanks. Right back.

             SABITHA exits.

EDITH: "You must not ask, it is forbidden for us to know, what fate has in store for me or for you."

             EDITH watches the lights come up on JOHANNA. She is wearing nicely fitted clothing. She sits in a chair and picks up her knitting. As she begins to work on her garment, a baby cries. She puts down the work and stands. KEN enters.

KEN: I'll go.

JOHANNA: Thanks.

             He exits.

KEN: *(From off.)* Come here.

        EDITH continues to watch. JOHANNA sits and picks up her knitting. She works while listening to KEN sing a lullaby. The baby settles down as the lights fade.

        The End.